CENGAGE Learning

Novels for Students, Volume 3 Copyright Notice

Copyright © 1998

Gale Research
835 Penobscot Building
645 Griswold St.
Detroit, MI 48226-4094

This book is printed on acid-free paper that meets the minimum requirements of American National Standard for Information Sciences—Permanence Paper for Printed Library Materials, ANSI Z39.48-1984.

ISBN 0-7876-2113-7
ISSN 1094-3552

Printed in the United States of America.
10 9 8 7 6 5 4

Annie John

Jamaica Kincaid 1985

Introduction

Ever since Jamaica Kincaid's work began appearing in *The New Yorker* magazine, it has excited critics and enthralled readers. Kincaid has been praised for her ability to tell the story of a girl attaining womanhood with all the emotion and beauty it deserves. Simultaneously, Kincaid expresses the significance and politics involved in that transition. Her second book, *Annie John* (1985), is comprised of short stories that first appeared in *The New Yorker*. Some critics consider *Annie John* a novel because the compilation of interwoven stories uncover the moral and psychological growth of the title character. This bildungsroman (coming-of-age story) has become Kincaid's best-known work to date.

Through Annie, Kincaid has brilliantly brought girlhood in the West Indies to literature as a masterful work of art. That art is a prose blend of European, American, and Caribbean folk forms of expression. The result is an effective rendering of a girl's struggle to discover her own identity. Annie is a girl growing up in an idyllic garden setting. At first she is the sole figure in that Eden—she has only her parents and Miss Maynard to interact with —and she maintains her sense of singularity when she finally begins mixing with others. Her omnipotent mother keeps the powers of the world and of death at a distance. Gradually, however, her mother introduces death and separation in order to mature Annie and prepare her for the world. The story of the mother creating the daughter is not unlike the works of Mary Shelley *(Frankenstein)* or John Milton *(Paradise Lost)* in the sense that the created becomes more than the creator intended.

Kincaid once said in an interview that her history began on ships and continues as corruption. By this she meant that the ideal human morality—which the Europeans tried to disseminate with empire—had instead become political, cultural, and moral corruption. That was the gift left behind as independence. Her island of Antigua is a microcosm of all newly independent colonies and the ensuing corruption. And Kincaid, like other West Indian people, is an amalgam of all who arrived at these islands by boat—Carib Indian, African, and Scottish. Kincaid explained this to Allan Vorda, for *The Mississippi Review* by telling how the library (from whence she stole books as a girl) that was ruined by an earthquake in 1974 would have been rebuilt by the colonial administrator. "Antigua used to be a place of standards. There was a sort of decency that it just doesn't have anymore. I think the tragedy of Antigua for me, when I began to see it again, was the loss of the library."

At the time of the earthquake, Kincaid was living in New York and she had recently taken up her name. She was born in Antigua May 25, 1949 as Elaine Potter Richardson, daughter of Annie Richardson and a father of whom she will not speak. When her family's economic situation made a turn for the worse, Kincaid dropped out of the university. At seventeen, she was sent to Westchester, New York, to work as an *au pair*, or nanny. Kincaid continued to pursue her education, however, and studied photography at the New School and later attended Franconia College in New Hampshire. In her early twenties, the desire to write became urgent but she did not think serious writing was being done anymore.

Dreading to be known, should her attempt to write fail, she fished about for a new name. She was not familiar with the black power movement or other African-American political groups and so did not choose an African name. Besides, she has often said, the only thing she has in common with Africa is her skin color. Her consciousness is a construct of the western hemisphere. Reflecting this consciousness, along with her view of her history as a blend of corruption and boats, she chose the name Jamaica. Jamaica is derived from *Xaymaca*, the translation Columbus made of the Carib Indian word for that island, translated again into English. She chose Kincaid because, as she told Allan Vorda, "it just seemed to go together with Jamaica."

Soon after becoming Jamaica Kincaid, her writing came to the attention of William Shawn, editor of the *The New Yorker*. She became a staff writer there in 1976 and married the editor's son, Allen Shawn. In 1983, her collection of stories titled, *At the Bottom of the River* won an American Academy Zabel award. Kincaid followed up *At the Bottom of the River* with *Annie John* in 1985. In addition to writing fiction, Kincaid has published *A Small Place*, about colonialism and tourism in Antigua. She also continues to write a gardening column.

Plot Summary

Jamaica Kincaid's *Annie John* tells the story of a girl's painful growth into young womanhood. Annie Victoria John, the narrator, progresses from a blissful childhood in Antigua, when she is the center of her mother's attention, to a trying adolescence filled with fierce maternal conflict, to her departure from Antigua for England at the age of seventeen.

Figures in the Distance

At ten, Annie does not know that children die until a young girl dies in Annie's mother's arms. Annie's mother (also named Annie John) must prepare the child for burial while Annie's father, Alexander, builds her coffin. Annie begins to see her mother's hands differently after this experience and, for a time, does not want to be touched by or look at them. Soon, after two more of her acquaintances die, Annie secretly begins to sneak to strangers' funerals. Then a humpbacked girl her own age dies. Annie runs to the girl's funeral after school, forgetting to pick up fish for dinner. She is caught lying to her mother about her mistake and must eat dinner alone and go to bed without a kiss. However, when in bed, her mother comes and kisses her anyway.

The Circling Hand

In the chapter's early pages, Annie describes her idyllic holidays when she and her mother bathe together and share her mother's activities. She describes her mother's trunk, in which she has kept all of Annie's possessions since birth. She sometimes tells Annie stories about each of the trunk's objects, delighting Annie, who revels in her mother's love. This life of "paradise" begins to falter, though, when Annie's body begins to change. Annie's mother now forces her to stop wearing dresses made from her mother's fabric and sends Annie to learn both manners and to play the piano, at which Annie fails through misbehavior. Then Annie accidentally catches her parents making love and stares at her mother's hand making circular motions on her father's back. That night, Annie behaves defiantly toward her mother for the first time and is silently sure she will never let her mother touch or kiss her again. The next day, though, she allows her mother to kiss her when she returns from her first day at her new school.

Gwen

When Annie first arrives at her new school, she is friendless and unsure of herself. After her teacher assigns them autobiographical essays to write, however, Annie shows she is the smartest girl in her class. She writes of a day she spent with her mother bathing nude in the sea. She lost sight of her mother and, afraid of the water, could not swim to find her.

When her mother returned, she comforted Annie, telling her she would never leave her. Annie later dreamt of this event, only her mother does not return in the dream. She told her mother of the dream and received comfort again. Annie moves many of the girls to tears with this story. She does not tell them, though, that the story's ending is fiction. In actuality, her mother responded to the nightmare by warning Annie against eating unripe fruit before bed. Later that day, Annie makes friends with Gweneth Joseph, and they become inseparable companions. Annie soon becomes the first of her friends to menstruate. At school recess, in a nook of old tombstones, she exhibits her menstruation to them and they comfort her. Annie returns home to her mother, whom she feels she no longer loves.

The Red Girl

In her continuing rebellion against her mother, Annie strikes up a secret friendship with the Red Girl, an unkept girl with red hair who loves to play marbles, a game forbidden by Annie's mother. Annie begins to see the Red Girl secretly, to play marbles, and to steal, hiding her treasures underneath the house. When caught with a marble, Annie lies that she does not play marbles. Her mother, not believing her, searches under the house for Annie's marble collection but cannot find it. After days of futile searching, she tells Annie a terrifying story of her own girlhood. Annie, moved by the story, almost tells the truth until she recognizes her mother's attempt to manipulate her. The Red Girl soon moves away, and Annie dreams of living with her on a deserted island, where they joyfully send misdirected ships crashing into rocks.

Columbus in Chains

During history class, Annie reads ahead to a picture of Columbus chained in the bottom of a ship. Annie loves this picture of the colonizer brought low, and she relates it to a story about her grandfather, Pa Chess, who was rendered immobile by an illness. Annie writes her mother's laughing response to Pa Chess's plight under Columbus's picture: "'The Great Man Can No Longer Just Get Up and Go.'" She is caught by her teacher and must copy Books I and II of John Milton's *Paradise Lost.* At home, Annie's misery is compounded when her mother disguises breadfruit, which Annie hates, as rice and then laughs about it.

Somewhere, Belgium

When fifteen, Annie feels an inexplicable misery that sits inside her like a "thimble that weighed worlds." She and her mother are constantly at odds, though they hide their conflicts from others. Annie has a recurring dream in which she thinks, "'My mother would kill me if she got the chance. I would kill my mother if I had the courage.'" Since she has always been taught that dreams are the same as real life, the dream's words haunt her. Annie daydreams of living alone in Belgium like Charlotte

Brontë, the author of *Jane Eyre*, her favorite novel. One day, while studying her reflection in a shop window, Annie is taunted by four boys. She recognizes one of them as a childhood playmate who once almost hanged himself accidentally while she just stood by watching and who made her sit naked on a red ants' nest. When she returns home, her mother scolds her for talking to the boys, saying she acted like a slut. Annie retorts in kind, then goes to her room. She thinks about the trunk under her bed, which makes her both long for her mother and wish her dead. When her father offers to build her some new furniture, Annie requests her own trunk.

The Long Rain

Despite a lack of clear symptoms, Annie falls ill for three and a half months and cannot leave her bed. Corresponding with her illness is an unusual period of heavy rains. Her illness distorts her perceptions, one time causing her to try to wash clean the imperfections in her framed photographs, ruining them. Annie's grandmother Ma Chess arrives and assures Annie's mother that the girl's sickness is not like her uncle Johnnie's, who died from a curse after laying two years in bed. Ma Chess, an obeah (or voodoo) woman, becomes Annie's primary caregiver. On the day the rains stop, Annie's illness disappears. During her illness, Annie has grown taller than her mother, and she now feels repulsed by the world in which she lives.

A Walk to the Jetty

Now seventeen and willing to go anywhere to escape Antigua, Annie is scheduled to leave for England to study nursing. She mentally sums up her life, concentrating on her relationship with her parents. She says a polite goodbye to Gwen, who will soon be married, something which Annie vows never to be. She then walks between her parents to the docks and surveys the world she is leaving, feeling both gladness and sharp pain. At her ship, she bids farewell to her parents, both crying with her mother and feeling suspicious of her. The novel ends with her in her cabin listening to the waves making "an unexpected sound, as if a vessel filled with liquid had been placed on its side and now was slowly emptying out."

Characters

Ma Chess

Grandmother embodies the traditions of the West Indies that Annie's mother abandoned when she left Dominica. Annie John's father's preference for Dr. Stephens indicates his desire to also leave these traditions behind. However, one day, Grandmother arrives and does not leave until Annie recovers.

Father

See Mr. Alexander John

Grandmother

See Ma Chess

Mr. Alexander John

Mr. Alexander John, Annie's father, is thirty-five years older than his wife and has many unacknowledged heirs. He is a carpenter builder who brings humorous tales about Mr. Oatie, his partner in the construction business, back to the lunch table. These daily reports have the effect of emphasizing the growing tension between mother and daughter. During the lunch routine, they behave properly to each other and Mother rarely fails to be amused by his stories. Mr. John represents the world of masculinity for which Annie's mother is preparing her. Until Annie is ushered into that world, however, it remains as distant as the haunting idea of boys playing marbles.

Mr. John built the family's house and made the furniture within. He protests against allowing the obeah woman to tend to Annie and he does not like Ma Chess. However, there is one moment of closeness between Annie and her father when he tells her of his own mother. Given the fears and obsession Annie has with her mother, this apparent empathy with Mr. John is actually a moment when Annie vicariously experiences the fantasy of being like her father—sleeping with mother until the age of eighteen when mother, then, conveniently dies.

Miss Annie Victoria John

The title character is a precocious young girl growing up in an Edenic garden governed by her loving mother. This changes with the onset of puberty and the declaration of independence her mother imposes on her. A civil war breaks out between them not unlike the Angelic war of *Paradise Lost*. The more Annie struggles to be distant and different from her mother the more alike they become. In the end, Annie leaves the island with her own trunk, calling to mind the exodus her mother made from Dominca years before.

As the narrator of the story, Annie is at liberty

to fabricate reality as she sees fit. Consequently, the line between myth or dream and reality is thin. She actively imitates her favorite literary personas, Satan and Jane Eyre, who moved into their own adult identities through rebellion and flight and recreated, in some way, the exact world from which they fled.

Annie also allows the traditional culture to exist with the present. She loves her grandmother and the magic her grandmother has. She is not afraid to give that as much importance as the magic of the schoolteacher and the doctor.

Finally, Annie dies to her childish self—the self that ruled the girls who gathered among the tombstones during recess and the child who hid marbles and stolen books beneath the house. This occurs during a three-month rain while she is ill. Recovery comes with the help of her grandmother and the realization that she is too large for her home —she is now literally taller than both her parents. Not only does she want to leave, she must leave as a necessary step in her formation as a woman. She must take her trunk and go to a new place and build her world there.

Mrs. Annie Victoria John

Having fallen out with her father at age sixteen, Mrs. John packed her yellow-and-green trunk and left Dominica for Antigua. The boat she left in was hit by a hurricane and was lost at sea for five days. The boat was a ruin but Mrs. John and her trunk were fine. Annie's baby clothes and memories are kept in this same trunk beneath her bed. It is fitting that the mother's trunk comes to be used in this way because, as she says to Annie, "I loved you best."

Mrs. John is the benevolent goddess governing the garden from which little Annie observes the funeral, observes death. The paradise cannot remain such forever and gradually the mother introduces death and separation. She has formed Annie and she sends Annie away.

Mother's position is typical of Caribbean women. The women run the households and the men are sent out to work. Consequently, the children are indistinguishable from the mother while she goes about her tasks until it is appropriate to give the children their own identities. But in *Annie John* this situation becomes abnormally tense because there is only one identity. Furthermore, there is only one name. The mother fights to give it away while Annie struggles to take it.

Ma Jolie

A local obeah woman reccomended by Ma Chess. Mother calls her to come administer to Annie. Ma Jolie does not know as much as Ma Chess, however, and can do little. She prescribes traditional medicines, places appropriate candles in the room, and pins a foul-smelling sachet to Annie's nightie. The obeah concoctions are set behind Dr. Stephen's on the shelf above Annie's bed.

Gweneth Joseph

She is the first girl at the new school to notice Annie. It is not long before the two girls fall in love and become inseparable. But, eventually, Annie becomes bored with Gwen and in the end comes to see Gwen as a silly, giggling, schoolgirl come to bid farewell. She tells Annie of her engagement and receives a humored blessing. Annie stands inwardly amazed that she ever loved Gwen.

Little Miss

See Miss Annie Victoria John

Mineu

Mineu is a playmate of Annie's and the only boy close to her age in the narrative. When together, Annie and Mineu liked to reenact local events. This play leads Mineu to fake his own hanging in order to imitate an actual hanging. Annie watches as it goes wrong. She is unable to move. Luckily a neighbor comes and saves the boy. Years later she meets him in the street. They simply say "hello." Meanwhile, his friends snicker and poke each other while Annie's mother catches sight of the scene. Later, her mother calls her a slut for talking to him.

Mother

See Mrs. Annie Victoria John

Red Girl

The Red Girl embodies the very antithesis of what Annie has been taught to be proper. They meet when the Red Girl climbs a tree to collect a guava in a manner normally reserved to boys. She is dirty, smelly, and plays marbles with the boys. Annie embraces and kisses her, as the ultimate rebellion against her mother's notions. It is the temptation of the Red Girl that leads Annie into a "series of betrayals of people and things."

Ruth

The daughter of the Anglican minister doesn't fare well in Antigua. Ruth is one of the few English children in the community. She is an embarrassed blonde who is frequently the class dunce. Annie thinks that Ruth would rather be home in England "where no one would remind her constantly of the terrible things her ancestors had done."

Dr. Stephens

The family doctor is an Englishman named Dr. Stephens. He represents modern science and has served the family through Annie's other illnesses— like hookworm. Mother agrees with his theory that germs need to be rooted out and destroyed. He represents modern science and is approved of by Mr. John, but his medicinal prescriptions prove ineffectual against Annie's debilitating depression.

Themes

Death

Death enters the frame of *Annie John* at the outset and never leaves. As a distant event observed by Annie, death serves as a counter reality to Annie's position as the beloved of her mother. Consequently, Annie's obsession with this other reality keeps the possibility of separation as the end of her blissful girlhood absolutely hidden. Death also serves to exaggerate the distance of the story and, thus, hide the narrator. In the first sentence, therefore, the adult narrator transforms into a girl fascinated by the apparently abstract concept of death.

There is a literal graveyard in the distance that Annie sees figures, not people per se, enter and leave. Death comes closer when Nalda, Sonia's mother, and then Miss Charlotte die. Annie is attentive to this facet of life and watches it. She observes funerals. She notes where death is. Yet she does not grieve. Annie wants to touch death by touching the hunched back of a dead girl whose funeral she attends for the purpose of observation. Disturbing Annie's peace, however, death nears her twice through the person of her mother who was holding Nalda and talking to Miss Charlotte when they died. These two events foreshadow the discovery of imperfection in Annie's universe.

Media Adaptations

- An audio cassette was madae of *Annie John* in 1994 by Airplay Inc.

Death does not come to Annie but she dies to three things: her girlhood, her mother, and her home. The first two take place through inevitable growth events. There is much that marks Annie as becoming a woman and, therefore, rivaling her mother for ownership of their shared name. The two primary events are her first menstruation and her illness. Her first menstruation is full of death images beyond the obvious significance of biological change—she faints because, she says, "I brought to my mind a clear picture of myself sitting at my desk in my own blood." Her illness is a mock death. When she comes forth from her sick bed she is taller and no longer seems to be of the Antiguan world.

Identity

The central struggle, or agon, in Annie's story is her struggle to bring forth her own identity. That identity is fulfilled through the scripted story of the trunk—she will have her identity when she leaves bearing her trunk. This struggle involves mood swings, rebellious adventures, the awakening of sexuality, and a coming to terms with historical reality. However, the person on whom this struggle is focused, and who has some responsibility in its instigation, is her mother. The mother-daughter tension dominates the work. The tension is not eased though Annie's struggle meets with success. She gains an identity despite her adult telling of her story—in which she clearly becomes a woman in her mother's image—actual reconciliation is absent. Annie's trunk carrying identity, then, is a death to her self and loss of her mother.

Life as a child is set up as Edenic. Annie is indistinguishable from her mother and happiness reigns. That is, until the day her mother says they are now separate. The demand for Annie to suddenly be independent, to have her own subjectivity, is the high of the book. It arrives in Chapter 2; the central image is that of her parents having sex and particularly "The Circling Hand" of her mother on her father's back. At that point, Annie says, "To say that I felt the earth swept away from under me would not be going too far." Her model of the universe—a dual universe with two beings in one dress fabric—had suddenly become a universe of independent bodies all doing their own things to their own ends. The rest of the work details the way in which Annie puts herself back together and finds her own reflection. She had been seeing herself as a smaller version of her mother but gradually she sees her own reflection in a shop window. She reminds herself of "Satan just recently cast out of heaven." Eventually, identity formation leads her to a figurative death. Her recovery from her illness is also her arrival at her identity as a woman. Recovered, she is taller, conscious of her power as a woman who knows herself, and with her new wisdom she sees she has outgrown the very island of Antigua.

Topics for Further Study

- Working from the example of Annie and her mother, what is the psychological make up of the family? Is there one working model or do we all have individual relationships?

- Compare how families—especially mothers—are portrayed in today's media with the novel's portrayal. Use examples of television sit-coms, cartoons, and movies for your findings.

- Think about Annie's illness and the help she received from the obeah woman; does your family use any home remedies? Ask your parents what their parents did for them when they were not feeling well and compare that with how your family currently treats illness.

- Research the politics of travel or photographic hunting. What, if any ethics are involved with the pursuit of recreation or game? What impact does the multi-billion-dollar tourism industry have on native peoples and the environment?

- Respond to the following excerpt from Kincaid's essay, *A Small Place:* "Have you ever wondered why it is that all we seemed to have learned from you is how to corrupt our society and how to be tyrants...? You came."

Annie uses several tools to form her identity. The first is her body. Her prowess and strength affords her respect from her classmates and captainship of the volleyball team. The other tool is her intellect. Being above average, she is not delinquent in opportunities to boost her confidence. But this does not prove as important as knowledge gained by observing people at home and hearing stories. One such story is of her mother's departure from Dominica. Annie knows the story well and, therefore, always has an example of strong womanhood before her. She also knows the story of her father, but she rejects his narrative although she empathizes with his tragedy. There are other narratives she rejects. Uncle John was a promising young man who died young. Annie notes that his belongings are kept in a trunk. Annie's things are in a trunk, too, but she decides to follow her mother's narrative and leave Antigua with a trunk—a new one—rather than follow the other narratives which both involve death. Re-enforcing her choice is Charlotte Brontë's story *of Jane Eyre*, whose heroine also strikes out on her own.

PostColonialism

Postcolonialism is a literary theory developed in response to the literature being written by people in countries previously governed by the British crown. In the years since the granting of independence, the people of these nations have had to reconcile their identity as educated British subjects with their awareness of their own subjugation by that government brought about by sudden self-determination. This resonates directly with Annie's identification with *Jane Eyre* as well as references to Milton and Shakespeare. Annie has been taught English literature—stories from the land of the former colonial administration. However, the postcolonial writer does not reject this literature; instead, she embraces it as her own. She also embraces the English tongue as her language, but now she will use them to tell her own story.

There are many references to the history of colonialism in *Annie John*, but two key moments involve a classmate named Ruth and Christopher Columbus. Both occur in Chapter 5, "Columbus in Chains," but resonate throughout the entire work. Being a good student with aspirations, Annie has trouble remembering the reality of her heritage or discerning whether she fits in "with the masters or the slaves—for it was all history, it was all in the past, and everybody behaved differently now." Still, there is some remembering and hard feelings over the past. Annie says of Ruth, "Perhaps she wanted to be in England, where no one would remind her [what] her ancestors had done."

Crucial to Annie's understanding of herself as a postcolonial subject is her crime against history. She is caught not paying attention to a history lesson, but she is punished for defacing her school-book in a way that was blasphemous. "I had gone too far this time," she says, "defaming one of the great men in history, Christopher Columbus, discoverer of the island that was my home." Annie is aware of how tenuous is the idea that this island is her home. She is here only as the curious result of Empire. Still, it is her home just as English culture is hers but with a little obeah thrown in.

Point of View

The first person ("I") retrospective narrative is constructed with episodes. The prime person in *Annie John* is, of course, Annie. Therefore, the Antigua shown the reader is that which is filtered through Annie. There are eight episodes highlighted in the chapter headings. During each episode more information is given about Annie. The timeline jumps but there is a steady progression from Annie as a young girl to her departure from home as a young woman.

This narrative, however, is ironic because an adult Annie establishes the reality of the story as if it was the perspective of little Annie. In other words, Annie knows her own story's outcome but tries not to reveal this. The novel opens by literally noticing figures in a distance and also by placing the story at a distance, "during the year I was ten." Thus the effort on the part of the young Annie to show her mother as an Old Testament deity is offset by the adult attempt to reconcile. The mother remains beautiful and loved though the literal story might say she is simply left behind.

Symbolism

The most important symbol of the work is the

trunk. Each of the characters has a trunk—a place where their identity formation blocks are kept. In the case of Uncle John, it is all that is left. For Annie, the trunk with all of her baby things is a fun thing to clean out because she then hears stories about herself. When she leaves Antigua, Annie— like her mother when she left Dominica—takes a new trunk to build a new life. Father has a trunk but it is not solid. Father's trunk is everywhere. It is made up of all the women and illegitimate children that Annie and her mother run into. It is made up of the house and furniture he built. He adds to this trunk daily with stories about work because there is no one who wants to tell his story—Mother is busy with Annie's story.

Irony

Irony is akin to an "inside joke." It occurs when the intended meaning is the opposite of what is actually said. Kincaid offers many wonderful moments of irony. One example is in Chapter 5, when Annie says that colonialism is past and now "all of us celebrate Queen Victoria's birthday." It is a rather sudden cultural reference in the midst of a paragraph about the past. Many things happen in the phrase. Annie has been saying that the past is behind them, yet they still celebrate some queen's birthday. She is also noting that the personification of colonialism (the reign of Queen Victoria was the heyday of the Empire) remains as a national holiday.

More of these ironic moments involve works of literature. For example, on the desk of Miss Nelson, an Englishwoman, is an elaborate edition of Shakespeare's play *The Tempest*. She is reading this work while the girls are writing their autobiographical essays. The irony is that on the one hand, the teacher is simply reading one of the great plays of English literature. The deeper implication is very complex because that play has become a grand touchstone for all postcolonial writers, especially those of the Caribbean. The reason is this: many intellectuals of those islands read that play as the moment of conquest, as if Shakespeare was writing the reality of colonialism into effect with his play. Further, the figure of Caliban—a person brought to the island to labor—mixes his identity with the spirit of the island, Sycorax. Caliban is a slave who has learned English so that he can curse his master. The children writing their essays are a result of the same process—brought to the island and now expected to peacefully get along with their former masters. Particularly, Annie's narrative involves her being stranded on a little island—like the characters in the play—but unable to call to her mother. She, like Caliban, yells at her master but there can be no understanding.

Dream Vision

Unlike the culture whose literature she adores (in *Jane Eyre*, for example, mythology has been banished from England), Annie does not divide the mythical from reality. Kincaid uses this in the narrative itself, so that dreams and myth are written in and make up her characters. The result of this is the legitimating of oral tradition. The first instance of this appears early in the novel and concerns the dead. Annie reports that "sometimes they showed up in a dream, but that wasn't so bad, because they usually only brought a warning." Another example of this technique comes when Kincaid has Annie recite her autobiographical essay. This essay is atypical because in some sense it is a very mature psychological metaphor but it also mythologizes the mother-daughter relationship. A final example is the event of Annie's and Mother's "black things," subjective demons, wrestling on the lunch table only to return—never to grapple again—to their rightful owners. This blending of realities validates dreaming as a way of thinking; it carries on the traditions represented by the obeah woman and Ma Chess.

Contact, Colonialism, and Independence

Originally inhabited by the Siboney people, the Island of Antigua, the setting for Kincaid's *Annie John*, was populated by Arawak and Carib Indians when Christopher Columbus arrived there during his second voyage in 1493. He named the island after a church in Sevilla, Spain, named Santa Maria de la Antigua. Thirty years later it became an outpost of the Spanish Conquistadors. In 1629, the French made a base there as Spanish power descended and the British had not yet taken control. French control was brief, however, and the English arrived in 1632. The Treaty of Breda formalized this situation in 1667.

From 1674 to 1834, the island was one large sugar plantation. Slaves were imported from Africa because the indigenous peoples fled or had been killed. The end of slavery brought freedom but no opportunity to be free. For the next hundred years, Antigua and surrounding islands were under the jurisdiction of one and then another federation. Greater independence was achieved in 1967, with statehood within the British Common-wealth granted in 1981. Finally the seven islands of the East Caribbean formed a merger. The single nation of the Organization of Eastern Caribbean States

(OECS) came into being in 1987 and included the former British colonies: Antigua, Barbados, Dominica, Grenada, Jamaica, Montserrat, St. Kitts-Nevis-Anguilla, St. Vincent, Tobago, and Trinidad.

Latin America and the Caribbean

The 1980s was a troubled decade for the nations of Latin America and the Caribbean. Warily, they attempted to cease being the playground and raw material supplier of Europe and America. In doing so, they strengthened old trading alliances and forged new ones. Meanwhile, the United States began to create NAFTA with Canada and Mexico, while Europe moved closer to unionization. In addition to economic competition, the United States practiced active interventionism.

Acting out of the Monroe Doctrine—that the United States will not tolerate interference by any European power (including Russia) in the affairs of the Western Hemisphere—and the precedent set by President Theodore Roosevelt, the United States intervened everywhere to both good and bad effect. In the late 1990s, the U.S. still enforced a trade embargo against Cuba that had been in effect since 1959. It may never be known just how involved the United States was in the turmoil that disrupted life in El Salvador and Nicaragua throughout the 1980s. Nor will the full story of Haiti's troubles be known. Less mysterious, however, were the invasions of Grenada in 1983 and Panama in 1989. In the first case, the Reagan administration acted in reaction to a coup, the potential endangerment of U.S. medical students, and the fear of even closer ties between Grenada and Cuba. The leader of Panama, on the other hand, was accused of laundering drug money. He was arrested in the invasion and began serving a sentence of forty years in the United States.

The 1980s in the United States

The decade of the eighties was original only in the way that culture in the United States sought to blend its past into the now. It was marked by pastiche, superficiality, recreations of old movie serials, nostalgia for a golden age that only ever existed on television, and "culture wars." The economy hummed at the surface with any sort of lifestyle and time available for consumption. Meanwhile, corporate mergers, downsizing, and an abrupt shift toward service economy left industrial America partially unemployed and the labor movement—beginning with the air-traffic controllers's strike of 1981—drastically weakened. To offset this industrial downsizing, the government embarked on an awesome weapons program. The result was an incomprehensible debt and a huge pile of nuclear warheads that nobody wants to ever, ever, use. It seemed to be a decade of deciding what to do—no clear answer has yet emerged.

Race Relations

The Civil Rights movement encountered a backlash in the 1980s for which it was unprepared.

Leaders of the movement knew the highpoint and victories of the 1960s were past but they could hardly believe that the Miami riots of 1980 announced a decade of violence. Membership in neo-Nazi and Ku Klux Klan groups rose while racially motivated hate-crimes increased in frequency. Normally tolerant environments, like college campuses, reflected this trend. The climate of the nation had suddenly become conservative.

Elections in the 1980s reflected the drastic change. Reverend Jesse Jackson, considered by many to be the successor to Martin Luther King Jr., ran twice for president in 1984 and 1988 as a Democrat. But the 1980s instead saw Republican President Ronald Reagan complete two terms of office that were succeeded by George Bush. Reagan won in a landslide because the populace felt that change might have occurred too fast. The brakes were applied and civil rights victories began to be overturned. In 1987, legendary civil rights activist and the first black to serve on the U.S. Supreme Court, Justice Thurgood Marshall, expressed his opinion that President Reagan was ranked at the bottom in terms of civil rights for all Americans, black or white. In a symbolic capping off of the decade, the elections of 1989 brought Republican David Duke, a former Ku Klux Klan grand wizard, to the Louisiana state legislature. Much to the relief of everyone, including the embarrassed Republican Party, Duke's bid for the U.S. Senate was unsuccessful.

Critical Overview

Response to *Annie John* has been unanimous in its praise. Reviewers focus on Kincaid's successful writing of a girl's coming of age as well as the wonder and excitement of a historic epicenter —the Caribbean. More serious views of the work simply explore this theme further by investigating the family as represented in the story and as existing in the West Indies. Critics have also noticed aspects of the novel which break new ground. For example, the harmony with which Kincaid treats the blending of obeah and modern medicine.

First reviews of the work in 1985 were excited, glowing, and attentive to Kincaid's prose ability. Paula Bonnell wrote in *The Boston Herald*, that the publication of Kincaid's first two books were "eagerly awaited events." Both, she continues, "are recreations of the self in that emotional country where dreams and what might have happened are part of the truest story of one's life." Jacqueline Austin agreed. She wrote a review in *VLS* months later saying, "Kincaid does write what she knows, what she knows is rare: pure passion, a past filled with curious events, a voice, and above all a craft." Austin also comments in passing about heritage. She names other writers from the West Indies to say that Kincaid is in a group trying to "encompass two traditions." She doesn't go much further nor does she say which two traditions. John Bemrose is more particular in his review for *Maclean's Magazine*. He says, "The instrument of Kincaid's success is a prose style whose subtly varied cadences suggest the slow, dignified pace of life in colonial Antigua. She also knows her way around the human heart." In the *Times Literary Supplement* in the fall of 1985, Ike Onwordi adds nothing new. He glosses over the fact that Kincaid's work is an "episodic" autobiography using "language that is poetic without affectation."

Heavier analysis of *Annie John* followed slowly. In 1990, H. Adlai Murdoch wrote an article for *Callaloo*, entitled, "Severing the (M)other Connection: The Representation of Cultural Identity in Jamaica Kincaid's *Annie John"* where he attempted to reconfigure the Oedipal tools of Freud for an utterly matriarchal order. Murdoch argues that as Caribbean writers began to create their own literature free of the burden of empire, they must confront the Oedipal tensions of identity formation. Such a reading assumes that the only route to the child's, or the newly independent nation's, subjectivity is by confrontation and overthrow of the father, or ruling power. Only then can the child own his culture, or mother. "The issue of subjectivity, beset with problems such as recognition of self and other and oedipal conflict under the most conventional circumstances, is complicated further here given the additional factors of colonialism and pluralism which continue to mark Caribbean society and culture." Fortunately, Murdoch does not belabor Freud's script but adds Lacan's notion of mirror as well as the more deconstructionist notion of phallic signifier.

Together they enable a reading in which Annie's mother is the main power broker against whom Annie struggles, as would the son against the father in traditional Freudian readings, to attain her independent subjectivity. This analysis stays within the realm of psychological interpretation despite its promise to link postcolonial facets as well.

More recent criticism reflects postcolonial theory and views Kincaid as a postcolonial writer. Bill Ahscroft, Gareth Griffiths, and Helen Tiffin wrote the book on postcolonialism in 1989—*The Empire Writes Back: Theory and Practice in PostColonial Literatures.* The theory arises out of the historical fact that English literature as a discipline arose concurrently with the pressures of Empire. Consequently, previously colonized people found themselves independent but speaking English. They were not returned to pre-colonialism. They had to create a new cultural identity at peace with the unpleasantness of colonialism and new sovereignty. With the realization of this phenomenon, critics like James Nagel reread Kincaid's *Annie John* as more than a bildungsroman coming of age story. Thus in his 1995 article, "Desperate Hopes, Desperate Lives: Depression and Self-Realization in Jamaica Kincaid's *Annie John* and Lucy," he builds upon Murdoch's insight. The mother becomes blended with the greater powers and the Oedipal constructs fracture beneath the pressure. The family's dynamics are now linked to the greater historical event that is Antigua.

Nagel notes the traditional bildungsroman

aspects of the novel and then includes the background: "a legacy of slavery and deprivation and the rich texture of Annie's family life ... as well as the English cultural overlay on the social patterns of Antigua ... the eminence of the Anglican Church ... European Christianity ... folk rituals of potions and curses... Everything in this society has a dual foundation, even the local dialect." The novel is seen here for its complexity and applauded for its ability to express the multiplicity of Antigua through the charm of a little girl. But that is art—to show how people live in their own circumstances. Allen Vorda quotes Henry Louis Gates saying this about Kincaid: "she never feels the necessity of claiming the existence of a black world or a female susceptibility. She assumes them both. I think its a distinct departure that she's making, and I think that more and more black American writers will assume their world the way that she does. So that we can get beyond the large theme of racism and get to the deeper themes of how black people love and cry and live and die. Which, after all, is what art is all about."

Beyond the areas where Kincaid subtly breaks new ground—as in her casual blending of traditional and modern medicine through the meeting of the obeah and pharmaceutical medicines —there is the serious craft that Gates describes. Kincaid's writing is wonderful and her story captivatingly emotional because, while she is expressing a political transformation, she focuses on the human effect—the effect on the little girl.

Sources

Bill Ashcroft, Gareth Griffiths, and Helen Tiffin, *The Empire Writes Back: Theory and Practice in Post-colonial Literatures.* London; Routledge, 1989.

Jacqueline Austin, "Up from Eden," in *VLS*, No. 34, April, 1985, pp. 6-7.

John Bemrose, "Growing Pains of Girlhood," in *Macleans Magazine*, Vol. 98, No. 20, May 20, 1985, p. 61.

Paula Bonnel, "'Annie' Travels to Second Childhood," in *The Boston Herald*, March 31, 1985, p. 126.

H. Adlai Murdoch, "Severing The (M)other Connection: The Representation of Cultural Identity in Jamaica Kincaid's *Annie John,*" *Callaloo*, Vol. 13, No. 2, Spring, 1990, pp. 325-40.

James Nagel, "Desperate Hopes, Desperate Lives; Depression and Self-Realization in Jamaica Kincaid's *Annie John* and *Lucy,*" *Traditions, Voices, and Dreams: The American Novel since the 1960s*, eds. Melvin J. Friedman and Ben Siegal. Newark: University of Delaware Press, 1995.

Ike Onwordi, "Wising up," in *The Times Literary Supplement*, No. 4313, November 29, 1985, p. 1374.

Allan Vorda, "Interview with Jamaica Kincaid,"

Mississippi Review Web Edition,
http://sushi.St.usm.edu/mrw/9604/kincaid.html,
1996.

For Further Study

John Bemrose, "Growing Pains of Girlhood," *Maclean's Magazine*, Vol. 98, No. 20, May 20, 1985, p. 61.

> In this complimentary review, Bemrose praises Kincaid's graceful style and her depiction of Annie John's resistance to the constraints of her environment.

Paula Bonnell, "'Annie' Travels to Second Childhood," *The Boston Herald*, March 31, 1985, p. 126.

> Bonnell commends Kincaid's rich rendering of life in Antigua and her ability to communicate the emotional reality of Annie John's struggles.

Selwyn R. Cudjoe, "Jamaica Kincaid and the Modernist Project: An Interview," in *Caribbean Women Writers: Essays from the First International Conference*, edited by Selwyn R. Cudjoe, Calaloux Publications, 1990, pp. 215-32.

> In this interview, Kincaid discusses her career, her familial relationships, Caribbean culture, and critical responses to her work. She specifically addresses the ending of *Annie John*.

Wendy Dutton, "Merge and Separate: Jamaica

Kincaid's Fiction," *World Literature Today*, Vol. 63, No. 3, Summer, 1989, pp. 406-10.

> Dutton explores the connections between *At the Bottom of the River* and *Annie John*, seeing them as complementary texts that together develop one cohesive story.

Moira Ferguson, *Colonialism and Gender Relations from Mary Wollstonecraft to Jamaica Kincaid: East Caribbean Connections*, Columbia University Press, 1994.

> Taking a grand historical view, Ferguson links Kincaid's work to the struggle over gender in English literature.

Moira Ferguson, *Jamaica Kincaid: Where the Land Meets the Body*, University Press of Virginia, 1994.

> Ferguson's book-length study investigates Kincaid's connections between motherhood and colonialism, the harsh tone these connections produce, and her protagonists' struggles for self-determination.

David Barry Gaspar, *Bondmen and Rebels: A Study of Master-Slave Relations in Antigua*, Duke University Press, 1993.

> Gaspar details the legacy of the colonial power dynamic in which Annie grows up.

Patricia Ismond, "Jamaica Kincaid: 'First They Must Be Children,'" in *World Literature Written in English*, Vol. 28, No. 2, Autumn, 1988, pp. 336-41.

> Comparing *Annie John* to various stories in *At the Bottom of the River*, Ismond explores relationships between mothers and daughters in Kincaid's work, as well as Kincaid's reliance on childhood perception and fantasy.

Jamaica Kincaid, *A Small Place*, Plume, 1989.

> Kincaid reflects on the place where she grew up and asks Western tourists to join her. In doing so, she reveals the Antigua tourists never see —the one without hospital and library.

H. Adlai Murdoch, "Severing the (M)other Connection: The Representation of Cultural Identity in Jamaica Kincaid's *Annie John*," *Callaloo*, Vol. 13, No. 2, Spring, 1990, pp. 325-40.

> Murdoch employs psychoanalytic concepts and Antiguan cultural conflicts to illuminate Annie John's rebellion against authority and her search for identity.

Roni Natov, "Mothers and Daughters: Jamaica Kincaid's Pre-Oedipal Narrative," *Children's Literature: Annual of the Modern Language Association Division of Children's Literature and*

The Children's Literature Association, Vol. 18, 1990, pp. 1-16.

> Natov explores Kincaid's use of imagery, particularly associated with Annie John's mother and with water, to illustrate Annie's changing relationships and perceptions.

Donna Perry, "Initiation in Jamaica Kincaid's *Annie John*," in *Caribbean Women Writers: Essays from the First International Conference*, edited by Selwyn R. Cudjoe, Calaloux Publications, 1990, pp. 245-53.

> Connecting Kincaid's novel with other works by women of color and Third World women, Perry relates the traditions of female storytelling, obeah, and intergenerational blood ties to Annie John's development.

Diane Simmons, *Jamaica Kincaid*, Twayne Publishers, 1994.

> Simmons' book-length study focuses on Kincaid's treatment of loss and betrayal in her works, as well as her use of obeah (the magical power of transformation) and the rhythm and repetition in her prose. Her chapter on *Annie John* includes a comparison to J. D. Salinger's *Catcher in the Rye*.

Marilyn Snell, "Jamaica Kincaid hates happy endings," an interview in *Mother Jones*,

September/October, 1997, pp. 28-31.

> Kincaid explains to Snell that she feels it is her duty to bring people down a bit from their oblivious happiness.

Helen Pyne Timothy, "Adolescent Rebellion and Gender Relations in *At the Bottom of the River* and *Annie John*," in *Caribbean Women Writers: Essays from the First International Conference*, edited by Selwyn R. Cudjoe, Calaloux, 1990, pp. 233-42.

> Timothy examines the links between Caribbean cultural practices and beliefs and Kincaid's treatment of mother-daughter conflicts.

Evelyn C. White, "Growing Up Black," *The Women's Review of Books*, Vol. III, No. 2, November, 1985, p. 11.

> White praises Kincaid's ability to evoke both life in Antigua and the painful struggles of adolescence. She contends that while Kincaid addresses colonialism, she foregrounds her young protagonist's internal dilemmas.

CPSIA information can be obtained
at www.ICGtesting.com
Printed in the USA
BVHW070420151221
624021BV00013B/1721